THE
LORD'S
PRAYER

IMAGINE IT
ANSWERED

DAN BOONE

dustjacket

ISBN: 978-1-937602-49-9

Dust Jacket Press
PO Box 721243
Oklahoma City, OK 73172

www.DustJacket.com
Info@DustJacket.com

Cover and Interior Design by D.E. West at ZAQ Designs

www.dustjacket.com

Dedication

To Bill Allen, a man whose love for the Ten Commandments and The Lord's Prayer have guided his life and business. May others follow your example.

Hallowed Be Your Name

It costs one million dollars to use the name *Krispy Kreme*. They are the best donuts this side of heaven. I'm convinced that angels own the recipe. Their melt-in-your-mouth creation is simply divine. A friend checked into the franchise price and discovered if you want to sell donuts called *Krispy Kreme*, the price tag is one million dollars. It is a million dollar name.

But compared to *Disney, Krispy Kreme* is pocket change. Last time I checked, Disney's name is worth fifteen million. You get the rights to the name with all the legal requirements attached. There are places you can and can't use the name. Things you can and can't do with it. If you pilfer, slander, or misuse the name, you will meet the well-heeled lawyers whose job it is to protect the use of the *Disney* name.

The creation and protection of a name brand is big business in our world. The handlers of John Edwards and Tiger Woods are working overtime to redeem the brand of these adulterers who ruined their name. John and Tiger have profaned their names by choices they made. The value of their name on a shirt, a golf club, or a political event has plummeted. Some of the products endorsed by Tiger dropped him. It was in the contract he signed. If he did anything to tarnish his name, the company was no longer obligated to be identified with him.

Name brand protection and use is a highly legal issue – from *Krispy Kreme* to *Disney* to Tiger Woods. Laws are involved. It is a serious thing to misuse or profane a name.

The Lord's Prayer begins with "Our Father in heaven, hallowed be your name." Now this should come as no surprise to us. We are the people of the 10 Commandments who know that, "You shall not take the name of the Lord your God in vain, for the Lord will not put up with any misuse of his name."[1] Again and again our scriptures warn us about profaning the name of God. Talk about name brand creation and protection…this is serious stuff. God's name is to be hallowed by his people. Another way of saying it is, "May your name be sanctified among us."

So how did we get God's name? When were we given the right to use it in the first place? Apparently we think we have the rights to the name.

> We've plastered it on our churches hospitals and schools.
> We sew it on our hoodies, handbags, and T-shirts.
> We've written it in songs, books, poems, and plays.
> We've attached it to our causes, actions, and appeals.
> We affix God's name to our opinions, decisions, and explanations.
> Political parties bless in God's name.
> Merchants and musicians sell in God's name.
> Nations pledge in God's name.

> How did we get God's name?

> He gave it to us.

You remember Moses standing in the wilderness before the burning bush. God is telling him to go tell Pharaoh to "Let my people go," and Moses says, "Who shall I say sent me?" If we were Moses today, we'd be looking into the bush asking, "Who are you? Are you a concept like peace or love or freedom? Are you the balance between yin and yang? Are you like The Force in Star Wars? Are you the next big thing like Google or iPhone? Are you a wave of the future? Are you magic? Who or what do I say sends me?"

And God answers Moses, "Tell Pharaoh that the verb 'to be' has sent you." God gives him the name "I am who I am" or "I was, am, and will be," which has become for us the name Yahweh – the God of action.

"Moses realizes that he is not in the presence of a concept, some amorphous blob of a spirit. He is face-to-face with a peculiar God who has peculiar ways of doing things. This God has heard the cry of oppressed people. This God has not only heard but has been moved to act. This God is bigger than kings like Pharaoh. This God chooses strange, inept people like Moses to help disrupt things at the palace. This God creates this God's own identity. This God is sovereign, free, untamed, compassionate, and holy." And when Moses got to Egypt and spoke in the name of this God,[2] things happened. Bloody water and frogs and gnats and flies and boils and thunder and hail and locusts and darkness and death and seas opening and water coming out of rocks and bread falling from the sky. People are liberated by the name of this holy God. Moses speaks the name and God does things. God happens all over Egypt.

There is massive power in the name – the kind of power we frail humans would like to get our hands on and use for our own purposes. Which is probably why when they got to the foot of the Mountain of Law, God said, "Don't take my name in vain. Don't use my name for what I am not doing."

"Thou shall not take the name of the Lord thy God in vain." For most of my life I thought this meant don't cuss. Don't use God's name with the word damn, or swear using the name of God in any way, or the name of any of the Trinity. And that would be one way to misuse the name of God, but I don't think this is why the commandment was given. I can't see a bunch of foul-mouthed Jews running around in the wilderness cussing a blue streak. Especially given the fact that they had just been liberated by this name, this God.

This means a lot more than cussing. We profane the name of God when we forge God's name to our wishes. A congregant once told me that God had told him that I should give him $100. God never bothered to tell me. An employee once announced to her boss that God had revealed to her that she was to be hired to do a specific task at a specific salary. And we all know of some religion major, dating far over his head, who announced to his date that God had told him that she would be his wife.

Silly, I know. But is it any more a misuse of the name of God than to announce that 9/11 was the judgment of God on America, or the tsunami in Bangladesh was God's judgment on Muslims, or the hurricane in Haiti was God's way of getting even for all the witch doctors in their country?

People write lots of opinion checks and forge them with God's name. This profanes the name of God.

And what about all the religious paraphernalia we sell with God's name on it? God rocks and God socks and Jesus bobble-head dolls and Jesus ink pens and Holy Spirit cruises and Holy Spirit teddy bears…is God really present in all that?

I've seen men take the scriptures about the husband being head of the wife and treat their spouse like a subservient human, and label it God. Wars have been fought in the name of God that had nothing to do with God. Prejudices have stood for centuries with God's will affixed to their rationale. Sexual abuse has occurred under the name of God.

Scandals have happened in ministries claiming to be God's doing. I've seen preachers bilk little old ladies out of scarce dollars in return for promised healing or a miracle, and label it God. I've seen students make excuses for sloppy work and label it God. I've seen people cheat other people in the name of God.

We get hold of this powerful name and use it for our own purposes without any thought of the character and mission of God. If we did that with *Krispy Kreme* or *Disney*, we'd be sued for all we're worth.

Apparently, the misuse of God's name was of concern to Jesus. A little later in the Sermon on the Mount we hear Jesus say, "Not everyone who says to me, 'Lord, Lord,' will enter the kingdom of heaven, but only one who does the will of my Father in heaven. On that day many will say to me, 'Lord, Lord, did we not prophesy in your name, and cast out demons in your name, and do many deeds of power in your name?' Then I will declare to them, 'I never knew you; go away from me, you evildoers.'"[3]

God's name is not to be used wrongly or taken lightly. We don't casually stick this name on our idea, product, or words. Unless we are sure that we are actually doing what God is doing, we do not affix His name to our agenda.

But before I pronounce the final sentence on all profaners of the name of God, I must confess that I have profaned the name of God – when I was un-God-like while bearing his name, when my responses were impolite, when my priorities were skewed, when my checkbook was more materialistic than generous, when my thoughts about enemies were vengeful, when my words were misleading. When our words and deeds profane the God we claim to serve, the name is not hallowed in us or among us.

And that's why we pray the prayer – "hallowed be your name." It is a petition of sorts that requires action from God.

But just what is it about a name that is so important?

Names carry within them the essence of the person. If my assistant says on the intercom, "Dan, LeBron James is here to see you," I have more than a collection of letters running through my mind. I have knowledge of a person with a history and traits and specific characteristics. If she says, "Diane Sawyer is on the phone," it means more than 14 letters comprising two words. I have expectations of the conversation. Character, image, essence is wrapped up in a name. A name comes with a full-bodied person, a reputation, a history. A name bears the essence of a person.

The essence of God is holiness. Holy means "in a category all by itself, unique, one-of-a-kind." The name of God has no equal. It is holy. Only God is essentially holy. I know we say holy smoke and holy cow and holy crap and holy moly and holy Toledo…but none of it is really holy unless God is in it. God is the only source of holiness and anything that participates in God is holy and anything that doesn't isn't.

So when Jesus says, "Pray like this – Our Father in heaven, hallowed be your name," he is leading us into the presence of the holy God, evoking that God in our life, and bringing that God to bear on all we are and do. The name of God will be hallowed or profaned by our life.

A college student was hanging around with some friends who were involved in some bad stuff. What they were doing was morally wrong. And rather than doing wrong, this student just left. The rest of the group stayed. People were hurt, names were ruined, and the consequences were severe. Why did he excuse himself from the group? Why did he walk away? What caused him to go against the grain of his friends? "Simple," he explained. "My grandparents were saints. They loved me and were proud of me. They sacrificed for me to attend a Christian university." And then he said, "I didn't want to ruin their name. I love them too much to do that."

We are the walking brands of the name we bear. As President of Trevecca Nazarene University, I am the walking brand of Trevecca whether I realize it or not. Our public relations groups, our athletic teams, our summer mission teams, our professors – they all bear the name and become the brand of the university. People draw their conclusions about Trevecca based on what they see in us.

That's why I loved Kyle Funke. His 33 ACT score could have landed him in almost any university. He was math-and-science smart. Kyle battled a disease that resulted in brain tumors. He would get chemotherapy and show up in class a few hours later. Kyle had the best friends, the best sense of humor, the strongest faith, the most courageous resilience. I went to Raleigh, North Carolina for his funeral. He never graduated, so we gave his parents the diploma – a degree in Character and Courage. I'd choose Kyle any day as the walking brand of Trevecca. He hallowed the name of God. And God was magnified in his life.

But God doesn't pick and choose a few stalwart ones among us to be the name bearers. All his children are the walking brand. Which makes me, at times, look heavenward and say, "What were you thinking?" Entrusting his name to the likes of us is an enormous risk. Certainly there should be divine *Disney*-like lawyers running around looking for mis-users of the name, hauling us into court, and passing judgment. Does our God realize what he is doing by branding us with his name in baptism, telling us to ask in his name, giving us his name as a label for our deeds?

Most gods protect their name brand by images made in their likeness, little replicas or statues. These "image brands" are inanimate – they can't mess the god up. Our God hallows his name by giving it to us, making us in his likeness and image. We are the people of Jesus, the body of this Christ, the likeness of this God. And we pray that when people see us, they see God present in us and with us. We are the walking brand. And it matters to God.

This is a radical prayer that will get even more radical. To ask that God's name is hallowed in us and among us is basically to pray that we be made holy, that our life be hallowed by the obvious presence of God.

Your Kingdom Come

Words can get us in trouble. Depending on where they are spoken, who is speaking them, and who they are spoken to – words can radically change our life.

Go on an airplane and say, "I have a bomb." Your life will be different. Stand in front of an altar with the one you love and say "For better for worse, for richer or poorer, I do." Raise your right hand in a court of law and say, "I solemnly swear to tell the truth." Words can rearrange life.

But I believe the most life-altering, radical, dangerous, consequential words we can say are recorded in the prayer that Jesus taught us to pray – "Your kingdom come, your will be done on earth as it is in heaven."

Now I know we can say these words without meaning them, and not much happens, except we get more used to praying things we don't really mean.

I think this is why most liturgies that call us to the Lord's Prayer say, "Let us be ever so bold as to pray…Our Father." Let us be bold? Let us be *ever so bold*? Have you ever thought of yourself as needing boldness to pray the Lord's Prayer?

It is not a prayer for timid people. It is a radical prayer for the overturn of the powers that rule the world. It is a prayer of unsettling. It seeks more substantial upheaval than Al Qaida. It is more revolutionary than the KKK, Hitler's regime, or American democracy. This prayer beckons God to make his rule tangible everywhere in every way, for the earth to become the place where what God wants is done. We are inviting a tiger out of the cage. And this tiger is not tame.

Have you ever wondered what the swift, immediate answer to this prayer would look like? Here's my guess:

> Wealth would be redistributed. And most of us reading this would have less.
>
> The military would be unnecessary. Think of what could be done with all the money. Weapons would become farm implements.
>
> Washington DC would no longer be the seat of world power.
>
> The meek would inherit the earth.
>
> The planet would be restored and redeemed from our pollution.
>
> The weak among us would be empowered.
>
> The proud and arrogant among us would come down.
>
> Justice would be done in the courts.
>
> Health care would be global, and the hungry fed.
>
> Education would not be for the privileged few but for everybody.
>
> Self rule would cease and God would be the only sovereign.

And this would only scratch the surface. The world will one day be radically changed when the kingdom comes in fullness and God's will is done on earth as it is done in heaven.

So we pray this boldly. Really?

Sadly, many of us have prayed this like it was surrender to fate. We tell God what we want, but realizing that God will ultimately get what he wants, we tag our prayer with a P.S. at the end – "nevertheless, thy kingdom come, thy will be done." It's kind of like a pious capitulation, a helpless surrender, a hopeless resignation to fate. It's as if the devout are drugged to repeat, "your kingdom come, your will be done." It is spiritual anesthesia to keep us from plotting with God for the redemption of the world.

We're like Forrest Gump speaking philosophically at the grave of Jenny.

"Jenny, I don't know if Momma was right or if, if it's Lieutenant Dan. I don't know if we each have a destiny, or if we're all just floating around accidental-like on a breeze, but I, I think maybe it's both. Maybe both is happening at the same time. I miss you, Jenny. If there's anything you need, I won't be far away."

Forrest is contemplating whether life is chance or choice. If it is chance…then we pray "thy will be done" as resignation to what is going to happen anyway. If it is choice, then we are tempted to think we are in charge of our lives, so we lobby God in prayer, and get God to endorse our agenda for success. Either it all depends on God or it all depends on us (plus some help from God). Maybe Forrest was right and it's a little of both. But mostly, life is the recognition that we are the creatures of a God who is still creating the future and he invites us into his work by praying dangerous prayers that put us in the middle of getting his will done on earth.

I am remembering Jesus in the Garden of Gethsemane. The cross is in front of him. He prefers not to go. He asks the Father to let this pass. He prays for the cross to be removed but finally realizes that it is the way of God. He prays, "Nevertheless, not my will but yours be done." You tell me. Is this passive resignation or willing participation? Is it caving in to God or plotting with God? Is it resigning to fate or creating the future?

Jesus did not leave the garden limping like a pre-fated being. He said to the disciples, "Get up. Let's go. My Father is up to something that involves me!" Pray this prayer and you have obligated yourself to radical obedience.

I love to go to Disney World. There is something magical about the place. *The Magic Kingdom*, they call it. Well, it is and it isn't. The kingdom of Disney is created by a particular way of doing things. The territory is defined. You know when you are entering it. It has a look, a feel, a style. Companies have studied the Disney philosophy and tried to replicate it. Everything is intentional. The people who work there go through discipleship training in Disney-dom. They know exactly what they should and should not do. They are the walking brands of Disney. They are radically obedient to its ways. If you are a Disney employee, much is required of you. There are lots of rules in the place. Disney doesn't just happen.

Neither does the kingdom of God. It is central to the message of Jesus. It is the core of his ministry. It is the heart of the gospel, if not the gospel itself. The disciples are being trained for life in the kingdom. Jesus comes proclaiming the kingdom of God and saying all kinds of things about the kingdom:

> It is among you.
> It will come.
> It is already here.
> Repent.
> Enter it.
> It begins small and insignificant like a mustard seed.
> It is like a pearl of great price or a treasure hidden in a field.
> Go get it.
> People who thought they could never get in are on the invitation list.
> Old wineskins can't hold it.
> It is like a rich man who gave his money to servants and left town.
> It is a like a party that the wrong people are invited to.
> When the sick are healed, it is here.
> When Satan is cast out, it is here.
> When Jesus is seen in the poor, the imprisoned, the needy, it has arrived.

This risky crazy prayer imagines the world through God's eyes and participates in making it that way. What makes the kingdom so radical is that when God's kingdom comes, ours ends. It is the end of self rule. God has not come to make some good suggestions or to lobby for his agenda. God has come to reign.

I'm amazed by the characters in the Bible who actually knew how dangerous Jesus was – the Sanhedrin, King Herod, Pontius Pilate, Caesar, and Satan. They knew that the kingdom of God was the end of them. They didn't want to kill Jesus because they disagreed with his ideas. They wanted to kill him because he had come to destroy their little kingdoms and bring their rule to an end.

I remember speaking in chapel on "A Biblical Basis for Abstinence from Alcohol." In short, if we love our neighbor who might be destroyed by alcohol, we might chose to abstain as an act of loving solidarity. At the end of the presentation I invited students to text me their questions or write them on a 3x5 card. I would answer them in chapel the next day. One student wrote anonymously, *"Yes, I'm 21 and I choose to go to this school and I choose to drink responsibly and socially. That's the underlying factor – my choice, my life, my walk, my convictions."*

In chapel the next day, I read the statement out loud with emphasis on certain words *"Yes, **I** am 21. **I** choose to go to this school. **I** choose to drink responsibly and socially. That's the underlying factor – **my** choice, **my** life, **my** walk, **my** convictions."* Then I replied as honestly and lovingly as I am capable of, *"It's very obvious. It's all about you. And if this continues to be the basic ethical position of your life, you will not be a follower of Jesus Christ. **My** and **I** are the only words that will matter to you. You could not more succinctly express the mantra of self-sovereignty. **You** will do what **you** want to do. **You** will rule your life. **You** are building **your** ethics based on what **you** want to do. **You** are **your** own boss. And that is the essence of sin. **Me** doing what **I** want to do. It is spelled s-**I**-n."*

The essence of Christianity is very different. "I am crucified with Christ, and I no longer live, but Christ lives in me. And the life I now live, I live by faith in the Son of God who loved me and died for me."[4] This is the core of Christianity. My answer may have been blunt, but I fear this student did not understand how non-Christian this was of thinking is.

Can a person be a responsible social drinker and still be a Christian? Yes. Can a person think like this (*I, me, my, mine*) and still be a Christian? No. This is what sin does to us. It blinds us. It settles us into a life that's all about me. I can rationalize any behavior I choose. *I, I, I, me, me, me, my, my, my*…that's the way life is. The most damaging thing for Christianity is that it has become a little private self-affirming experience with God. That is not Christianity. The most important lesson of life is to learn that God is God and I am not. This messes with our self-rule and self-sovereignty.

Barbara Brown Taylor tells the story of a loggerhead turtle. The turtle had made its way from the ocean to the beach to lay her eggs in a sand nest. After watching for a while, Barbara left, so as not to disturb the turtle. The next day, she noticed that the tracks of the turtle led, not toward the ocean, but into the blistering dunes. As she followed the tracks, she found the turtle exhausted and nearly baked. Finding a park ranger with a jeep, she watched him set out to rescue the turtle. She writes,

> *As I watched in horror, he flipped her over on her back, wrapped tire chains around her front legs, and hooked the chains to the trailer hitch on his jeep. Then he took off, yanking her body*

forward so fast that her open mouth filled with sand and then disappeared underneath her as her neck bent so far I feared it would break.

The ranger hauled her over the dunes and down onto the beach; I followed the path that the prow of her shell cut in the sand. At ocean's edge, he unhooked her and turned her right side up again. She lay motionless in the surf as the water lapped at her body, washing the sand from her eyes and making her skin shine again.

Then a particularly large wave broke over her, and she lifted her head slightly, moving her back legs as she did. As I watched, she revived. Every fresh wave brought her life back to her until one of them made her light enough to find a foothold and push off, back into the water that was her home.

Watching her swim slowly away and remembering her nightmare ride through the dunes, I noted that it is sometimes hard to tell whether you are being killed or saved by the hands that turn your life upside down.[5]

Do we really want to pray the Lord's Prayer? "Lord, turn my life upside down, hook your Jeep to my shell of a life, pull me where you are headed, involve me in your work, and resurrect me for the life you intended."

We resist the pull of the kingdom in so many ways. We tie ourselves to the kingdoms of this world to keep from being tugged into the kingdom of God. Raniero Cantalamessa writes about the love of God as an ebbing sea which comes ashore to sweep us into the love that exists in the Trinity. This wave of love *"flows onto the beach at high tide and draws into itself whatever is on the beach with its receding waves. Some boats, however, are bounded on all sides or tied to a post in the ground. The sea surrounds them and caresses them, as though inviting them to follow. For a little while, the boats are lifted up and float, but since they are tied, they do not follow the sea as it recedes. They stay on shore, while other boats that are not tied put out into the deep under the sun on the tranquil sea."* [6]

We are tied to our habits, our possessions, our fears, our kingdoms. For brief moments we float in surrender to the kingdom coming ashore, but when it moves toward the deep, we resist going along. We are created to float in the sea of surrender to God's love, but we choose instead to be bound to the shore.

The prayer of "kingdom come" is the prayer to be completely yielded to God. It is letting go into God, going with God, releasing control to God. And when this happens, the kingdom comes, and God's will is done – not according to fate or by the power of personal choice, but by the activity of the Spirit working in us to do God's will.

And in the resurrection of Jesus, the kingdom of God is already being realized. Jesus is God's move to make everything new. Do you see the kingdom? I do…

I see the kingdom in our response to earthquakes in Haiti, Chile and Japan.

I see the kingdom when biology students plant gardens for the elderly.

I see the kingdom at work as college students tutor inner city kids in math and reading.

I see the kingdom when people make micro loans to entrepreneurs in India.

I see the kingdom when the International Justice Mission fights human trafficking.

I see the kingdom in a small church that builds a well in a poor village instead of giving expensive Christmas presents to each other.

I see the kingdom when Millard, suffering from Parkinson's disease, walks to the nursing home and sings to his wife, Barbara, who doesn't know him anymore because of Alzheimer's.

I see the kingdom when Chris plants an American Chestnut Tree, extinct from blight, but being resurrected.

I see the kingdom when Sam battles leukemia, and ends up encouraging all of us.

I see the kingdom when one of you forgives another one of you.

I see the kingdom when you kneel in surrender to God and get up to participate in the future of God.

One day, this kingdom will come in its fullness. But that doesn't mean it isn't already here.

Our Daily Bread

"Give us this day our daily bread." With this simple phrase, a massive transition happens in the Lord's Prayer. We move from the omnipotence of God to the impotence of humans. The prayer begins with recognition of

An intimate Father in heaven
A powerful name given to us
The hallowing of God's name in our lives
A kingdom coming to us
God's will being done on earth as it is in heaven.

After all this exalted language about God in his holiness and power and rule and sovereignty, the prayer now says meekly, "we need bread."

In these words we move from an omnipotent God to frail humans…which bothers some of us. We'd rather think more highly of ourselves. Words like *frail* and *needy* and *hungry* don't sit too well when we are trying to prop up our little self-sovereign kingdoms so we can …

> impress folk with our abilities
> and possessions
> and athletic prowess
> and smarts
> and stuff.

> But to be human is to be needy.

The story of our creation in Genesis 2 says that *"The Lord made Adam from the dust of the earth and breathed into his nostrils the breath of life and he became a living being."* [7] I am enthralled by two Hebrew words in this verse – *ruach* and *nephesh*.

Ruach means breath. The Lord shaped this claymation character into a body, leaned over it, put his mouth over the creature's nose, and blew. Dust + *ruach* = human. This breath is our life. No wonder we call the third person of the Trinity *"the Holy Ruach"*. The Spirit is the life-giving, life-sustaining wind of God that animated a valley of dry bones, resurrected the dead Jesus, and was blown into the church on the Day of Pentecost. We live by divine breath, as individuals and as the collective body of Christ.

The second Hebrew word makes it even more interesting. When God breathed into us the *ruach* of life, we became a living *nephesh*. The word is translated *soul* or *being*. The root of this word is the part of the human body identified as the neck or throat. The neck is the most vulnerable part of our body. It is fragile and can be broken. Conquered peoples bared the back of their necks to the one who conquered them. To bend the neck before another is to confess weakness and vulnerability.

Part of the neck, the throat is the passageway through which everything we needed for life passes – air, water, and food. The throat is our reminder that we are emptiness inside, begging for life-sustaining resources from the outside. God has created a passageway for us to receive the nourishment we require.

Whether you interpret *nephesh* as vulnerability, need, or emptiness, it is obvious that we are fragile beings. God breathed his life into our nostrils and we became needy humans, living thirsts, walking hungers, perpetual needs.

To pray, "give us this day our daily bread," is to be deeply in touch with our essence, to declare that we are needy humans before our Creator. The most perfect of all creatures is one who has capacity for being filled with God, by God…and knows it.

One of my favorite movies is "What About Bob?" Bob Wiley, played by Bill Murray, is a very needy human. He has every disease and phobia known to humankind. He is so needy that he has driven his counselor nuts and is looking for a new one. He finds Dr. Leo Marvin, played by Richard Dreyfus, a psychiatrist who has an inflated ego. Dr. Marvin has just written a best-selling book titled "Baby Steps," revealing a therapy that will cure all human ills. Bob sees Dr. Marvin, and latches onto him as someone who can help him. Bob believes "Baby Steps" is the miracle cure he has been looking for. But at the end of the first session, Dr. Marvin announces to Bob that he will be going on vacation and will not be able to see Bob for several weeks. Soon Bob's paranoia kicks in and he tries to find out where Dr. Marvin has gone. By deceit, he learns that the good doctor is vacationing with his family at Lake Winnipesaukee. And Bob boards a bus to go there.

In a move of theological genius, the writers of the movie have Bob board the bus with his goldfish, a smaller creature that is dependent on Bob for fresh oxygenated water. The fish is named Gill. Get the theology? Gill is how a fish breathes. Breath (*ruach*) is at stake for the fish… and for Bob. As Bob de-boards the bus, Dr. Marvin happens to be coming out of the local grocery store. He tries to escape without being seen, but to no avail. Bob chases him down on the Main Street sidewalk. Dr. Marvin immediately begins to chide him for violating his vacation. Bob falls to his knees on the sidewalk and says the most profoundly honest thing that humans can say – "I need, I need, I need."

This is what we are doing in this petition of the Lord's Prayer – declaring with Bob that we are needy creatures before the One we believe can help us.

Bread is a powerful Biblical image for human neediness. The scriptures are full of bread stories – feeding the multitude, breaking bread with disciples, eating with sinners, Jesus the Bread of Life. But one of the most revealing bread stories is in Exodus 16.

The people of God have been in Egypt working as Pharaoh's slaves. They've been there 400 years, working 12 hours a day, seven days a week, 52 weeks a year. It has been a long haul, and Egypt is all they know. Egypt is about scarcity – not having enough. They've always had to scrap for what they could get while others had more than enough. Nothing has ever come to them as gift. They earned every grain of bread they ate.

Finally, by way of plagues and open seas, they are delivered from the land of Egypt and begin to move through the wilderness toward the Promised Land. Behind them is the glory of the empire with the guarantee of scarce provisions under an oppressive Pharaoh. Ahead of them is wide open wilderness without any provision at all. They travel awhile and reality sets in. They are stranded between Egypt where their dreams died and the Promised Land of hope. And they have run out of food. No bread, no meat, no water.

Wilderness is the name of a place. It becomes symbolic of any place where you find yourself with not enough, where you can't save yourself, where you come face to face with your need. Wilderness has many faces.

Plummeting house values.
All the good jobs leaving town.
A relationship that is draining you.
A body that won't work right.
Fizzled finances in the college registration line
Hyper-dependent relatives.
Shrinking retirement funds.
A GPA that won't get you where you need to go.
A marriage that seems hopeless.
A habit that is destroying you.

Wilderness isn't far from here, and for some of you, it is your current mailing address.

So what did the people of God do in this situation? They griped and complained to high heaven. Can you hear them?

"If only we had died in Egypt…at least we had food there."

"Moses has no clue where he's going. He's brought us into the wilderness to kill us all."

"At least we had food and water in Egypt. Let's go back. God doesn't care about us."

Waaaa, waaaa, waaaa – call the wambulance. The title of this chapter in the annals of the people of God might be "The Days of Whine at Moses."

They blamed Moses, they blamed God, they griped and griped and griped – which is one way to deal with our neediness. They learned it in Egypt where complaining was the daily dish. And now they are rehearsing it in the wilderness. But God is trying to get Egypt out of them so he can make a new people.

And then…God's love comes trickling down in the form of bread. They ask, "What is it?" which is the Hebrew word *manhue*, or manna. So they just called the bread "What is it?" College students have done the same standing in a cafeteria line looking at today's mystery dish. They say, "What is it?" I say, "Right, manna."

These liberated slaves had never before received bread as a free gift falling from the sky. They had always worked for their bread, controlled its production, scrounged for more. And here in the barren wilderness, it comes falling down from heaven without them doing anything. This is not Egypt.

It's a wonder, a miracle, a gift. It is not scarcity. It's abundance. And the scripture tells us that everybody had enough. They were not used to that. They were used to some having a little and some having a lot and some having none. But here, everybody had enough.

But the scarcity of Egypt was so deep in them, they began to hoard the bread. They stockpiled it. They collected more than enough. And it began to turn sour and rot… because you cannot keep God's generosity for yourself.

So Moses told them to stop hoarding, and to practice Sabbath. Gather manna six days and rest on the seventh.

What they gathered on day six would not spoil, and would carry them through day seven when they did not go out manna picking. Pharaoh would never have given them free bread, much less a day to rest. God commanded it.

Those who live under Egypt's scarcity will never have enough, so they will work-work-work to collect more-more-more to secure themselves so that they will never be needy. This is what Egypt does to us. It robs us of our humanity. We start believing that it is a bad thing to be needy so we anxiously stockpile manna to secure ourselves in this world of scarce resources. We don't pray "I need bread" – we work ourselves to death thinking we must make our own manna.

The time comes when they get through the wilderness and start growing their own food – but they never forget that it is the abundant gift of God, and they rest on Sabbath to help them remember that God is the ultimate source of bread.

Dr. Leo Marvin is Egypt personified – the guy with the best-selling book and all the right answers. By the end of the movie, Dr. Marvin is comatose in a psych ward, muttering gibberish, totally dependent on professional caregivers. But Bob Wiley has become a loving, gracious, delightful human who is grateful for the gifts of acceptance and grace that have come his way. He is surrounded by people who love him and is a helper to his fellow humans as…a counselor.

> Dr. Marvin tried to be god. Bob tried to be human.
> Dr. Marvin lived in Egypt. Bob lived in the
>   Promised Land.
> Dr. Marvin believed in scarcity. Bob believed in
>   abundance.
> Dr. Marvin griped and complained his way
>   through life.
> Bob was grateful for each gift.

Mature believers are deeply aware of their neediness and are deeply grateful for all they have received.

Forgive Us, As We Forgive

We become profoundly human when we realize that we pray, "Give us this day our daily bread." We become even more human when we are willing to confess that we were wrong, that we have sinned, and that we need forgiveness.

Asking for forgiveness humbles us. It places us at the mercy of another who is empowered to forgive or withhold forgiveness. God has given us the assurance that if we confess our sins, he is faithful and just to forgive us. Not everyone has offered us the same deal.

I suppose the prayer would be easier to pray if it stopped with "Forgive us our trespasses," but it goes on to say, "…as we forgive those who trespass against us." What does that mean? That God won't forgive us until we forgive our offender? That we must earn forgiveness from God by forgiving those who sinned against us? That we have to sweep these horrible wrongs under the rug and look the other way as if it never happened… or God won't forgive us?

I've always believed that these interpretations of forgiveness actually do great damage to the justice of God.

I don't think forgiveness is meant to dull our capacity to be angry at sinful behavior. Biblical justice matters, especially if the kingdom of God is to come among us.

Let begin with the wrongs people have done to us. This is not where the prayer starts. It starts with the wrong we have done to God and others, but for discussion sake, let's say someone has really sinned against you – lied about you, stolen from you, taken advantage of you, raped you, cheated on you, intentionally hurt you – and any other bad sins you wish to name. Is the Lord's Prayer saying that we must forgive, forget, and go on as if nothing happened? No.

Before we can think of forgiving a bully, a brute, or a beast, we need to thank God for the grace to be angry. We need to get our arms around the reality of Biblical justice. This is not how God intended it to be. Making nice and acting like it didn't hurt does not work. And it hinders the kind of peace-making that God is after.

The first step in forgiveness is to acknowledge that wrong has been done to you, and that you are angry about it. I find great comfort in Paul's instruction to the Ephesians when he says, "Be angry, but don't sin."[8] That's all the permission I need to be genuinely bothered about what was done to me. This is good anger, the anger that calls sin what it is, stands for Biblical justice, and is willing to confront rather than let it slide. Once we get this right, we can now move toward forgiveness, not as the end of anger, but as the transformation of our anger for the good of the person who wronged us. Anger liberates us from denial. Forgiveness moves the relationship toward restoration rather than destruction. Does this make sense to you?

Now let me go a step farther. In forgiving this person, I don't think we excuse the person for what was done. We do not personally experience God's forgiveness until and unless we repent. God's posture is forgiveness. This is a finished act, completed in the cross and resurrection of Jesus. If we confess our sins, he is faithful and just to forgive us. God has already decided to forgive, provided the forgiveness, taken the posture of forgiveness, and promised it to us – BUT – until we confess the sin, we cannot experience the forgiveness of God. Neither can the person who has wronged us be forgiven until they seek forgiveness by acknowledging the wrong.

I remember the first time I kissed my wife Denise. It was several dates into our budding relationship. I had dreamed about it, hoped for it. I even caught myself practicing the kiss at the bathroom mirror. Lame, I know. It takes two to experience a kiss. For one to say, "I stand ready to kiss you" is movement in the right direction. But if the other is not leaning into the kiss, there no kiss. It takes two for the experience to be enjoyed.

We stand ready to forgive the offender, but forgiveness is not realized until the one who did us wrong leans into the kiss of forgiveness, enabling a restored relationship. Am I saying that we are to carry a grudge and withhold forgiveness from the jerk until he/she fesses up? No. We are to forgive as God forgives, which means that we are to take in our hearts a posture of willingness to forgive the offender. We no longer hold this person in our mental jail, waiting to appear in our court of judgment. We no longer grill them over the fire of our anger. We no longer carry them around in judgment, trying to get them to admit wrong, hating them, or despising them. Instead, we turn them over to God for justice to be done. We, like God, stand pre-determined to forgive them. But revenge and justice belong to God. We release them to God for God to do with them as God sees fit – believing that God is both just and merciful.

Christians are called to live into forgiveness willingly, even as God is graciously forgiving. Then we can go on without a brooding judgmental spirit. We release the prisoner to God realizing that if we had not, the prisoner would have become us. It is a horrible thing to be imprisoned by what someone has done to you. In Christ, we lay this burden down. It's like unloading a 50 pound back pack after a 15 mile hike. We can lay it down, live with our self, and work to repair the damage done.

But there is still another connection in the prayer between being forgiven by God and being forgiving toward others.

> *Forgive us our*
> *debts/trespasses/sins*
> *as we forgive our*
> *debtors/trespassers/sinners.*

In the Matthew version of the Lord's Prayer, there is even a PS about this. "For if you forgive others their trespasses, your Heavenly Father will also forgive you: but if you do not forgive others, neither will your Father forgive your trespasses."[9]

What is being said here? Sometimes scripture is the best commentary on scripture. Jesus tells a remarkable parable in Matthew 18:21-35. Peter is asking Jesus how many times he has to forgive one of the brothers for sinning against him. He even suggests the answer: seven times. Since seven is the perfect, whole, complete number, this ought to be enough.

Jesus should congratulate him on being so magnanimously forgiving. The Pharisees drew the line at three, then ka-pow! But Jesus raised the ante on Peter's 7. Not seven times, but 77 times – a lot more than seven.

But the real answer to Peter's question is not in the number, but in the parable that follows. It goes like this: A king decides to collect on all his *debts*, and calls in all his *debtors* – same word as in the Lord's Prayer. A man comes in who owes the king 10,000 talents. Pause for a little math. One talent was the equivalent of about 15 years of fulltime salary. So this guy will need to work 150,000 years and turn over every red cent to liquidate the debt. The people who were hearing the parable knew that this was mathematically impossible. This guy owed more than the entire wealth of nations in that day. It's like saying the President of the United States called you into his Oval Office and demanded that you pay off the national debt.

Well, our friend in the parable is in a long line of debtors and his turn comes. His name is read and the amount owed announced - let's make it an even $10 million. He says, "King, I don't have it. I can't pay." And the king coldly, without even looking up, says to the guards, "Liquidate him. Sell his wife, his kids, his house. Big garage sale, everything goes. And throw him in prison until he can pay off the balance. Next."

Swift – fair – just. He owes. He can't pay. He's history. And the guy falls to his knees and says to the king, "Have patience with me and I will pay you everything." The Greek word for what he is asking is *makrothumason*. It is translated *patience*. It's what an oldie but goodie song from my youth was talking about – "Give Me Just a Little More Time."

And the king does three unbelievable things:
1. He had compassion on the servant.
2. He cancelled the entire debt.
3. He let him go free.

Remember, this is a parable. Peter is still standing there with his question hanging in the air – "How many times do I have to forgive this person?" And Jesus answers Peter with a snapshot of a Father who is like a king who cancels unrepayable debt.

We remember this God. We've seen this God before. We've read about him in Psalm 103.

> *The Lord is merciful and gracious,*
>   *slow to anger and abounding in steadfast love.*
> *He will not always accuse,*
>   *nor will he keep his anger for ever.*
> *He does not deal with us according to our sins,*
>   *nor repay us according to our iniquities.*
> *For as the heavens are high above the earth,*
>   *so great is his steadfast love towards those who fear him;*
>   *as far as the east is from the west,*
>   *so far he removes our transgressions from us.*
> *As a father has compassion for his children,*
>   *so the Lord has compassion for those who fear him.*
> *For he knows how we were made;*
>   *he remembers that we are dust.[10]*

What a portrait of a forgiving Father! This should be permanently etched on our memory walls. But pictures don't always reveal everything.

Over our fireplace we have a family portrait. All 12 of us are in it – four married couples and four grandchildren. It was taken in the fall in our back yard. We are all dressed casual. I had just come from a Tennessee Titans/ Indianapolis Colts football game. I had on jeans, sweat shirt, and white socks. I was sitting cross-legged on the ground for the family photo. Denise did not like the idea of my white socks shining brilliantly in the middle of the picture. So I gathered fall leaves and piled them around my feet, hiding the white socks from the lens of the camera. But my white socks are not the only hidden things in the picture. There are baby bottles, pacifiers, ball caps, and diaper bags strategically hidden behind the backs of spouses. The messy stuff is all hidden.

It's easy for us to look at this parable and see a king loaded with the wealth of the world. He won't miss it if this guy can't pay. He's like the Texas oil tycoon who gets in his big Cadillac El Dorado with steer horns on the hood, and drives out to the far edge of his thousand acre spread, struts over to a struggling share cropper, and announces with his thick Texas drawl, "I'm gonna give you this little plot of land you've been farming," and then gets back in his Cadillac and drives off into the sunset.

Don't take that picture of God. Beneath the regal robe of this forgiving king is a cross-shaped scar, a hidden reminder of the cost of forgiveness. It is not obvious in the parable, but it is an essential part of the portrait. His own Son said from a cross of injustice, "Father, forgive them. They don't know what they are doing."[11] Most of the time I think we did know what we were doing, but he died for us anyway.

The king cancelled the debt. Set the servant free. Let's follow him and see what he does:

> *But that same slave, as he went out, came*
> *upon one of his fellow slaves who owed him a*
> *hundred denarii (about $20 bucks); and seizing*
> *him by the throat, he said, "Pay what you owe."*
> *Then his fellow-slave fell down and pleaded*
> *with him, "Have patience with me, and I will*
> *pay you." But he refused; then he went and threw*
> *him into prison until he would pay the debt.*[12]

There he goes. Uptight, hard-charging, clenched teeth, buttonholing people, exacting his due, collecting. No one gets away with anything. He has his little black book of IOU's. He's collecting from everyone who owes him. He sees a guy who owes him $20. After he collects from him that will leave him 9 million, 999 thousand, 980 bucks to go. That's 49,999 more people he needs to collect $20 from and he'll have his $10 million for the king. And he intends to do it.

Wouldn't you love to be this guy's spouse, friend, roommate, date, employee, son, or daughter? Some of you are.

He's living like he still owes the debt, and if he has to pay, so does everyone else. The saddest thing about the story is that he didn't hear what the king said – he doesn't know that he is forgiven. The guy thought he had gotten what he asked for – *makrothumason* – more time to repay the debt. He has a brother by the throat demanding $20 bucks or else. This small debt is repayable, given a little more time. This wrong can be righted. But instead of compassion and *makrothumason*, he delivers swift, immediate justice. Off to jail you go brother.

And look what happens next in the parable:

> *When his fellow-slaves saw what had happened,*
> *they were greatly distressed, and they went and*
> *reported to their lord all that had taken place.*
> *Then his lord summoned him and said to him,*
> *"You wicked slave! I forgave you all that debt*
> *because you pleaded with me. Should you not have*
> *had mercy on your fellow-slave, as I had mercy on*
> *you?" And in anger his lord handed him over to*
> *be tortured until he should pay his entire debt.*[13]

The refusal to forgive is too great a torture for humans to bear. It is a self-imposed prison.

When the king forgave the debt, he walked away owing nothing – almost. He did owe something. Something that only the forgiven can repay. Something that the Lord's Prayer is calling us to. What we owe God for our forgiveness is *resemblance* – to forgive as he has forgiven us. The people expected this man to reflect the grace he had received from the king toward his fellow humans. When they saw no resemblance, they knew this was wrong.

The parable ends… *"Should you not have had mercy on your fellow-slave, as I had mercy on you?" And in anger his lord handed him over to be tortured until he should pay his entire debt. So my heavenly Father will also do to every one of you, if you do not forgive your brother or sister from your heart."*[14]

It's a parable. Peter is still standing there with his question,

Lord, how many times must I forgive…?
Well Peter, there once was a king.
But Lord, he really owes me.
I know he does. Just like you owe the Father.
But Lord, there are all these $20 IOUs.
Yes, and there is the matter of the 10 million.

Finally Peter crawls under his nickname. The only people who can afford to never forgive… are the people who never sin.

What's the status of your little black IOU book? Is it filled with names of those who lied about you, stole from you, took advantage of you, raped you, cheated on you, intentionally hurt you? Hear me carefully. Be angry. What was done to you was not right in the sight of God. But do not live into your anger. Release this person into the hands of God for God to do with them what mercy and justice does. And be set free to forgive as God has forgiven you.

You are empowered by the Spirit of God to resemble God by taking the posture of forgiveness.

Lead Us Not Into Temptation... Deliver Us From Evil

By the time we get to the end of the Lord's Prayer, we begin to realize how needy we are.

Feed us our daily bread,
forgive us our wrongs,
keep us from the temptations of the evil one.

And if we have prayed the first part of the prayer seriously – that God's name would be hallowed in the way we live, and that God's kingdom would come through us, and that God's will would be done among us – then we have signed up for a battle with evil. We have become part of the struggle of Jesus against the principalities and powers of this dark world. We really do need God to keep us from walking blindly into temptation and to deliver us from the powers that are dead set on destroying us.

Evil is an interesting thing. It can be personalized, and is, in scripture. We meet the Devil, Satan, Beelzebub, Lucifer, the Father of Lies, the Accuser of the Brethren, the Dragon, the Sea Beast, the Ruler of Chaos, the Prince of Darkness. The evil one has lots of names and descriptions. But evil is also impersonal. It exists as ideologies, institutions, and entities. It is corporate – Hitler's Reich, the KKK, Islamic Fundamentalism, human trafficking – to name a few. But it doesn't stop there. Corporate evil has its roots in the economy, Madison Avenue advertising, technology, Wall Street, race groups, gender groups, the alcohol industry, governments, Hollywood. You can find the devil about anywhere you look – including the church. Powers are at work in these places to steal, kill, and destroy.

This is why Paul tells us that our struggle as the people of Jesus is not merely against flesh and blood, but against the rulers, the authorities, against the cosmic powers of this present darkness, against the spiritual forces of evil. It's why Peter tells us that the devil is a roaring lion, looking for someone to devour. It's why John writes that we will be persecuted in this world. And it's why Jesus teaches us to pray that we not walk into temptation blindly, but be delivered from the evil one.

There are probably three dangerous positions you can take on evil:

1. *Evil is a myth. It doesn't exist. All this hype about the boogie man is just to scare us into being better. This position is too light.*

2. *Evil is everywhere. There's a devil behind every bush, he's under your pew, he's gonna get you. This position is too heavy.*

3. *Evil doesn't faze me because I'm above it. This position is stupid.*

Evil is real. I not only believe there is a devil, I've met him/her lots of times. But evil need not be given a lot of attention, made over, or talked about. Just sign on with Jesus to destroy the works of the devil and you'll have your hands full.

This prayer is not suggesting that God is trying to lead us into temptation, but if we say "please don't lead me into temptation," then maybe he won't. God has no interest in steering us into the devil's trap. If anything, the prayer is asking that we not be led into traps unaware of the way evil is at work in the world.

So let's have some fun. If you want to study evil, the best place to go in scripture is the Book of Revelation, properly titled The Revelation of Jesus to John. In this last book of our Bible, evil is caricatured exquisitely. John the Revelator would have been an awesome movie producer. His images are phenomenal. In the Revelation, evil is portrayed as a red dragon chasing a pregnant woman, a beast that comes out of the sea, and a land beast who goes around telling lies about the sea beast thereby getting people to receive the mark of that beast on their forehead. But the epitome of the description of evil comes toward the end of the book in chapters 17–19. It's like John is leading us through an art gallery which has three paintings that graphically depict the situation of the people of God as they face the evil one. The art gallery might well be called, the Gallery of Destruction. Let's look at the three portraits.

The First Painting: The Great Prostitute

One of the seven angels who had the seven bowls came and said to me, 'Come, I will show you the punishment of the great prostitute who sits on many waters. With her the kings of the earth committed adultery and the inhabitants of the earth were intoxicated with the wine of her adulteries." Then the angel carried me away in the Spirit into a desert. There I saw a woman sitting on a scarlet beast that was covered with blasphemous names and had seven heads and ten horns. The woman was dressed in purple and scarlet, and was glittering with gold, precious stones and pearls. She held a golden cup in her hand, filled with abominable things and the filth of her adulteries. This title was written on her forehead: MYSTERY BABYLON THE GREAT, THE MOTHER OF PROSTITUTES AND OF THE ABOMINATIONS OF THE EARTH. I saw that the woman was drunk with the blood of the saints, the blood of those who bore testimony to Jesus.[15]

The Great Prostitute is impressive. She looks like she just walked out of Saks Fifth Avenue, dressed in purple and scarlet, the finest threads of the day. This lady is no Wal-Mart shopper. She wears gold, pearls, and gemstones. She is sassy. She is the mother of all prostitutes. Her limousine is a beast. She rides sidesaddle, tipsy from drinking the blood of martyred saints. She is arrogant, smooth, wealthy, powerful, cultured, and luxurious. She has everything she wants, and she flaunts it. Her clientele is impressive – kings, merchants, shipping magnates. The leaders of the world are recorded in her little black book. They have staked their lives on her ability to satisfy them.

And John says, "When I saw her, I was astonished… greatly amazed." You would be too. Evil rarely looks ugly when we first see it. In the Revelation, the Roman Empire is this elegantly seductive prostitute, impressive enough to catch John's eye. Introduce a dirty old street woman with wrinkled skin and matted hair, and we wouldn't take a second glance. The dark side always puts its best foot forward, hooking our desires and reeling us in. The guide of the gallery, John the Revelator, is now moving to the next room and the next painting. Let's follow him.

The Second Painting: The Pimp

I will tell you the mystery of the woman, and of the beast with seven heads and ten horns that carries her. The beast that you saw was, and is not, and is about to ascend from the bottomless pit and go to destruction. And the inhabitants of the earth, whose names have not been written in the book of life from the foundation of the world, will be amazed when they see the beast, because it was and is not and is to come.[16]

In one of my pastorates, I learned a lot about prostitution. Seductively dressed women walked the street in front of our church. Sometimes they'd come in for water or to get out of the cold. Each prostitute is only the tip of the iceberg. Behind her is a powerful pimp, the enforcer who protects her turf and sees to it that all the clients pay. Evil is never free. The pimp furnishes the prostitute with lies, luxury, and legal services. He pumps her ego, disguises her body, and uses her for his profit.

Rome had a pimp, the best in the business. This pimp had sponsored other famous prostitutes in scripture – Egypt and Babylon, to name a couple of famous ones. He used them up and left them in ruins. (You can read about the demise of Egypt in Exodus 12:29–14:30 and about Babylon in Isaiah 46–47.) Now the pimp has Rome.

One of the street prostitutes came to my study one day and told me she wanted out. She was tired of selling herself. When I suggested that she just quit, fear seized her. "He'll kill me. He's already broken girls' arms and noses. Nobody quits." I called a church 500 miles away and arranged for them to meet her at the bus station. She left to pack her things and say good-bye to a few friends. She would meet me back at the church and I would drive her to the bus station. She never showed. I never saw her again. I've often wondered if her pimp got wind of her plans.

In John's drama, the pimp-beast turns on the prostitute and devours her. Why? Because she got in a fight with a slaughtered Lamb and lost. She's used up. So now the beast is done with her. *"The beast and the ten horns you saw will hate the prostitute. They will bring her to ruin and leave her naked; they will eat her flesh and burn her with fire…The woman you saw is the great city that rules over the kings of the earth."*[17] The picture continues:

> *After this I saw another angel coming down from heaven,*
> *   having great authority; and the earth was made bright*
> *   with his splendor.*
> *He called out with a mighty voice,*
> *   "Fallen, fallen is Babylon the great!*
> *   It has become a dwelling place of demons,*
> *   a haunt of every foul and hateful bird,*
> *   a haunt of every foul and hateful beast.*
> *   For all the nations have drunk of the wine of the wrath*
> *   of her fornication, and the kings of the earth have*
> *   committed fornication with her, and the merchants*
> *   of the earth have grown rich from the power of*
> *   her luxury."*
> *Then I heard another voice from heaven saying,*
> *   "Come out of her, my people,*
> *   so that you do not take part in her sins,*

> *and so that you do not share in her plagues;*
> *for her sins are heaped high as heaven,*
> *and God has remembered her iniquities.*
> *Render to her as she herself has rendered,*
> *and repay her double for her deeds;*
> *mix a double draught for her in the cup she mixed.*
> *As she glorified herself and lived luxuriously,*
> *so give her a like measure of torment and grief.*
> *Since in her heart she says,*
> *"I rule as a queen; I am no widow,*
> *and I will never see grief,"*
> *therefore her plagues will come in a single day –*
> *pestilence and mourning and famine –*
> *and she will be burned with fire;*
> *for mighty is the Lord God who judges her."[18]*

Evil turns on its own. It destroys its carriers. Evil uses and discards. And God allows it to happen. Evil is incomplete. It cannot finish what it starts. Yet it cannot complete its mission of destruction because God stands in the way. So evil unleashes its fury on its carriers.

The announcement of the prostitute's demise has come. Rome, once powerful, seductive, mesmerizing, is now a buzzard-infested place of doom, decay, and demons. The enticement is gone. Evil always comes to its end – ruined civilizations, worn-out ideas, failed philosophies, empty lifestyles. Rubble lies where the glorious city once stood. The prostitute cannot defeat the Lamb, because in dying, the Lamb exposes the prostitute as a carrier of death. The collapse is catastrophic.

But in the middle of the crash, God shows up. God calls to the clients of the prostitute, "Come out of her, my people, so that you do not take part in her sins, and so that you do not share in her plagues" (v. 4). God is at work here, delivering us from evil. Our guide is ready to take us into the next room.

The Third Painting: The Clients in the Little Black Book

Alas, alas, the great city, Babylon, the mighty city! For in one hour your judgment has come…The fruit for which your soul longed has gone from you, and all your dainties and your splendor are lost to you, never to be found again!…Alas, alas, the great city, clothed in fine linen, in purple and scarlet, adorned with gold, with jewels, and with pearls! For in one hour all this wealth has been laid waste!"[19]

The final scene lists the devastated clients, those whose names were found in the prostitute's little black book. Kings, CEOs, politicians, real estate agents, merchants, grocers, car dealers, department store managers, golfers, clerks, hair stylists, advertising agents, athletes, pastors, military personnel, truckers, computer programmers, teachers, students, scientists – that would be the list if John were writing to our century.

Their world has crashed. It has gone up in smoke. The devastated clients stand before the ruins. They mourn, wail, grieve, and throw dust on their heads. They say, "*Alas, alas.*" I can't remember the last time I heard someone say "*Alas, alas,*" but I can remember the last time I heard somebody cuss. I think "*Alas, alas*" was about the same as cussing back then. "*Alas, alas*" was the "*damn it*" of today.

I've started listening more carefully to people who cuss. I think they are saying more about themselves than they realize. There is a theology of evil at work in cussing. You know all the four-letter words. People use them to express despair, frustration, and emptiness. Life is not turning out as they'd hoped; their dreams have been crushed. They feel used and abandoned. "G-D" is their way of declaring that God would not let them have what they wanted. The F-word says they feel like a piece of meat, unvalued, unloved – just used. They've been trashed, and they don't mind trashing others. And when they use the name of Jesus Christ as a curse, they are identifying the Lamb who defeated their prostitute and would not let them rule. They are naming the One whose death revealed their chosen darkness.

It's not a pretty picture. The scene ends with a poem of emptiness:

> With such violence Babylon the great city will be thrown
>   down, and will be found no more;
> and the sound of harpists and minstrels and of flutists
>   and trumpeters will be heard in you no more;
> and an artisan of any trade will be found in you no more;
> and the sound of the millstone will be heard in you no
> more; and the light of a lamp will shine in you no more;
> and the voice of bridegroom and bride will be heard in
>   you no more; for your merchants were the magnates
>   of the earth,
> and all nations were deceived by your sorcery.
> And in you was found the blood of prophets and of saints,
> and of all who have been slaughtered on earth".[20]

Our gallery is depressing – the destruction of cities and peoples by evil. We who have lived long in cities know what darkness can do to a place.

Our tour of John's Gallery of Destruction is over. We are sad that God does not have some alternative to this, some competing beauty with which to attract the world to himself.

And before we know it, John's tour guide is moving again. Is there another portrait for us to see in this dark gallery? As we move into another room, the light is almost blinding. After all this darkness of evil we are greeted by sheer illumination. Before us is a new portrait. It is a painting of people who have been delivered from evil, people who have been beaten and bashed by the beast, people ridiculed by the prostitute, people who resisted, people who refused to be assimilated into darkness.

> *And they are singing…*
>   *Hallelujah! Salvation and glory and power belong to*
>   *our God, for true and just are his judgments.*
>   *He has condemned the great prostitute who corrupted*
>   *the earth by her adulteries,*
>   *He has avenged on her the blood of his servants.*
>   *Praise our God, all you his servants,*
>   *You who fear him, both small and great!…*
>   *Hallelujah! For our Lord God Almighty reigns.*
>   *Let us rejoice and be glad and give him glory!*
>   *For the wedding of the Lamb has come,*
>   *and his bride has made herself ready.*
>   *Fine linen, bright and clean, was given her to wear.*[21]

Wow! We're seeing and hearing a wedding song. The Lamb has a bride, a beautiful bride. Her beauty doesn't come from the powder and plastic of a prostitute, but from the grace in her lover's eyes. Her attraction is not lustful seduction, but vibrant life. Her Master is not a powerful beast, but a risen Lord. Her destiny is not ruin, but a banquet. Her clothes are not cheap and racy, but pure and white.

She is singing on her wedding day. And for the life of me, she looks just like all of you. And she seems to be singing the last line of the Lord's Prayer…"For thine is the kingdom, and the power, and the glory forever. Amen."

DAN BOONE

The Lord's Prayer: Group Guide

I'm excited that you've chosen to use *The Lord's Prayer* in a group setting. Whether this discussion group is part of an established small group, a Sunday School class, or a new book group, it's my hope and prayer that the following guide will help you craft meaningful discussions aimed at gaining a better understanding of the Lord's Prayer. Below you'll find a guide that will help you make your group as effective as possible.

AT THE FIRST MEETING: Begin by getting to know each other. The first group meeting might be a dinner or social time in which you begin to set up group expectations and specifics like meeting time and meeting place. Also work on establishing group goals such as:

- To encourage consistent and passionate participation from group members.
- To gain new understanding of the Lord's Prayer.
- To create a safe group environment where members can relax and openly share thoughts and ideas.
- To pray together as a community in Jesus Christ.

PRIOR TO MEETING: You will find thoughtful group discussion questions that will help you dig deeper into the topic of each session. All group members should do their best to complete the corresponding reading prior to the meeting time to help foster the best possible discussion Also, group members might want to look over the discussion questions ahead of time, so they are familiar with them.

DURING THE MEETING: Most group sessions will have the following four components:

- Social time (catching up on each other's lives)
- Prayer time (sharing prayer requests and praises)
- Curriculum time (going through the book)
- Discussion time (reading and answering the discussion questions)

Your group might like to begin with social time or end with it. They might also like to add some worship time into the group meeting. As a group, you can discuss what format is most comfortable for you, and then settle into a routine so that group members will know what to expect. Finally, plan to begin and end on time, so that group members feel their time is respected.

AFTER THE MEETING: Complete your reading for the next group session and pray! Take time to pray for group members and their requests. Pray also for God to speak to you through your reading the next time the group is together.

Hallowed Be Your Name

1. What brand names mean a lot to you, and why? What names have been soiled for you, and why?

2. What evidence do we have that there is "massive power in the name?" What evidence shows up in the Bible? What evidence shows up today?

3. Discuss what is meant by the statement, "People write lots of opinion checks and forge them with God's name. This profanes the name of God."

4. Why do you think we humans are so tempted to use the name of God for our own purposes and opinions? What damage does this do?

5. How are you doing at being a name bearer for God? Does it excite you or scare you that God has entrusted his name to you?

Take time this week to pray that God would help you to honor his name through you.

Your Kingdom Come

1. Have you ever thought of yourself needing boldness to pray the Lord's Prayer? Why or why not?

2. What has your reaction been to praying "your kingdom come" been in the past? Fear? Excitement? Dread? Apathy? Hope? Hopeless? Discuss your varying reactions as a group.

3. What is the relationship between praying this prayer and ending selfishness?

4. Is this part of the Lord's Prayer one that we hold at a distance or reserve for others, as if asking, "Let your kingdom come for them, the ones over there, who need it?" Is this a hard part of the prayer for you to personalize? Why or why not?

5. In what way is the kingdom of God already here? What role do we play in this?

As you go throughout your week, keep the following quote in mind. And dare to pray with boldness, "your kingdom come."

"Life is the recognition that we are the creatures of a God who is still creating the future and he invites us into his work by praying dangerous prayers that put us right in the middle of getting his will done on earth."

Our Daily Bread

1. How easy is it for you to express your needs to others? To God?

2. What do you think about the statement, "to be human is to be needy"? How is this contrary to what the popular culture is teaching us?

3. Share one of your current or past "wilderness" experiences with the group. How does your attitude towards others and God change when you are journeying through a "wilderness" time?

4. How does our perspective change when we see life as a gift from God?

5. In what ways do you find yourself trying to secure yourself in this world (aka "stockpiling manna")? In what ways are you learning to respond to God's grace by being more gracious to others?

This week reflect on what it means to embrace your neediness, to see life as a gift, and to be grateful for all that God has given you.

Forgive Us, As We Forgive

1. Is it easier for you to seek forgiveness from those whom you have wronged or to offer forgiveness to those who have wronged you? Why do you think you answered the way you did?

2. Do you agree with the statement, "I don't think forgiveness is meant to dull our capacity to be angry at sinful behavior"? Why or why not?

3. In what way is getting angry the first step to the peace-making He desires?

4. Is forgiveness the same as reconciliation?

5. What is our role in forgiveness? What is our role in justice? What is God's role in forgiveness and in justice?

6. Is there someone or some situation that you need to release to God? How can the group pray for you?

As you move throughout your week, take on the posture of forgiveness, and see how your relationships with those around you and with God change.

Lead Us Not Into Temptation, But Deliver Us From Evil

1. Which type of evil do you identify with the most: personal evil, impersonal evil, corporate evil, or economic evil?

2. Of the three dangerous positions you can take on evil, which one do you most easily find yourself

taking? (Evil is a myth; Evil is everywhere; Evil doesn't faze me because I'm above it.)

3. Discuss the following quote as a group. "Evil rarely looks ugly when we first see it...The dark side always puts its best foot forward, hooking our desires and reeling us in."

4. How do we see the competing beauties of evil and God being played out in today's world?

5. What do you think it means that God stands in the way of evil's completion? What does this knowledge do for you as a Christian?

Pray that God will help you recognize and avoid evil. Ask him to strengthen you in the face of temptation.

DAN BOONE

Endnotes

[1] Exodus 20: 7 (NRSV)

[2] Willimon, William and Hauerwas, Stanley. Lord, Teach Us to Pray: The Lord"s Prayer and the Christian Life, Nashville: Abington Press, 1996, p. 42-43.

[3] Matthew 7:21-23 (NRSV)

[4] Galatians 2:20 (NRSV)

[5] Taylor, Barbara Brown. "Preaching the Terrors." Leadership Magazine (Spring 1992), p. 43.

[6] Cantalamessa, Raneiro. Contemplating the Trinity: The Path to Abundant Christian Life. The Word Among Us Press, Ijamsville, MD. 2007. p.53

[7] Genesis 2:7 (NRSV)

[8] Ephesians 4:26 (NRSV)

[9] Matthew 6:15 (NRSV)

[10] Psalm 103:8-14 (NRSV)

[11] Luke 23:24 The Message

[12] Mt. 18:28-30 (NRSV)

[13] Mt. 18:31-34 (NRSV)

[14] Mt. 18:34-35 (NRSV)

[15] Rev. 17:1-6 (NIV)

[16] Rev. 17:7-8 (NRSV)

[17] Rev. 17:16-18 (NIV)

[18] Rev. 18:1-8(NRSV)

[19] Rev. 18:10, 14, 16-17 (NRSV)

[20] Rev. 18:21-24 (NRSV)

[21] Rev. 19:1b-2, 5b, 6b-8 (NIV)

 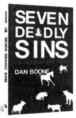